You Got This.

ISBN: 979-8-9888781-1-7
© 2023 Kimberly Elder. All rights reserved. No portion of this book may be reproduced in any form without permission from the publisher, except as permitted by U.S. copyright law.

How to use this workbook:

STEP 1: Set a Timer, Circle the Day, Mark the Time and Date
A timer let's you decide how long you need. Knowing the day, time, and date helps you discover patterns of feeling comfortable and uncomfortable.

STEP 2: Begin to Breathe
Breathing is one of the best ways to calm your body. Breathe through your nose or mouth, whatever feels best for you.

STEP 3: Read, Color, Calm
Make time for positive self-talk. Reading, tracing, and coloring can help you conquer negative thoughts.

STEP 4: Mindful Maze
Grounding exercises pull you to the present moment. Trace the maze with a pen or finger.

STEP 5: How Are You Feeling?
If you can figure out how you're feeling, you can recover and grow.

STEP 6: Reflect and Connect
Explore triggers and move forward with a plan.

Extra Time? Try to Draw, Doodle, or Journal!
This page allows you to explore feelings through pictures or words and connect with gratitude.

BONUS! The back of the book has extra grounding ideas and journal pages!

reset my mindset

TODAY: _____

Circle the day:

MONDAY TUESDAY WEDNESDAY THURSDAY FRIDAY
SATURDAY SUNDAY

What time is it? _____

SET A TIMER

 5 mins

 3 mins  10 mins

BEGIN TO BREATHE

- Shoulders Still
- Breathe in
- Breathe out
- Trace the rainbow

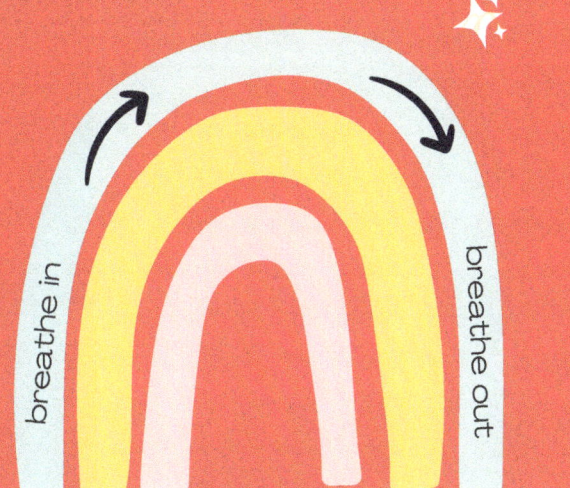

READ, COLOR, CALM

I CAN CONTROL MY CALM

MINDFUL MAZE

HOW ARE YOU FEELING?

REFLECT AND CONNECT

- Am I **H**ungry, **A**ntsy, **L**onely, **T**ired?
- What can I do?

READY TO RETURN _____   NEED MORE TIME _____

Draw or write what you are feeling.

What made you happy today?

-
-
-

reset my mindset

TODAY: _____

Circle the day:

MONDAY TUESDAY WEDNESDAY THURSDAY FRIDAY
SATURDAY SUNDAY

What time is it?_____

SET A TIMER

 5 mins

 3 mins  10 mins

BEGIN TO BREATHE

- Shoulders Still
- Breathe in
- Breathe out
- Trace the rainbow

 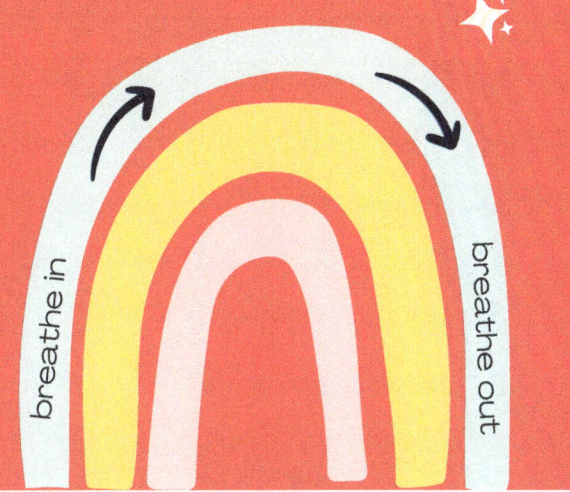

READ, COLOR, CALM

I CAN CONTROL MY CALM

MINDFUL MAZE

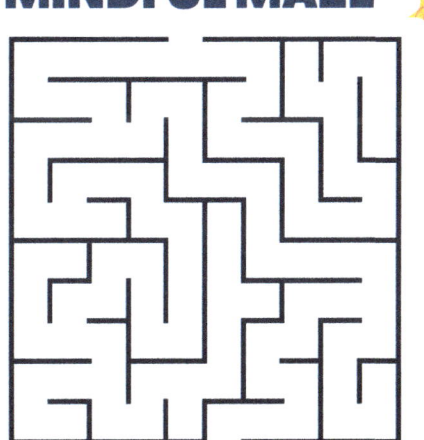

HOW ARE YOU FEELING?

REFLECT AND CONNECT

✋ Am I **H**ungry, **A**ntsy, **L**onely, **T**ired?

- What can I do?

READY TO RETURN_____   NEED MORE TIME_____

Draw or write what you are feeling.

What made you happy today?

-
-
-

reset my mindset

TODAY: _____

Circle the day:

MONDAY TUESDAY WEDNESDAY THURSDAY FRIDAY
SATURDAY SUNDAY

What time is it?_____

SET A TIMER

 5 mins

 3 mins  10 mins

BEGIN TO BREATHE

- Shoulders Still
- Breathe in
- Breathe out
- Trace the rainbow

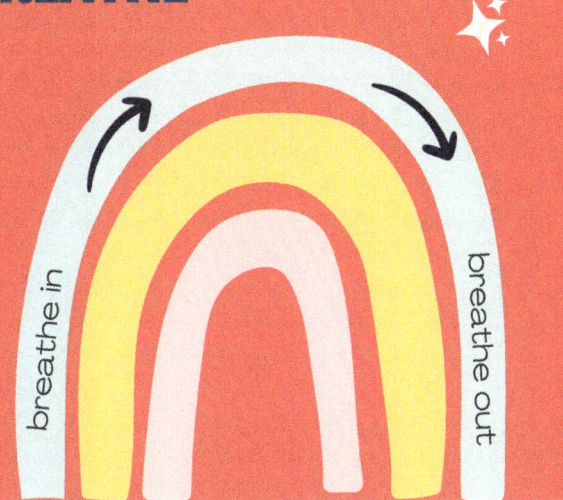

READ, COLOR, CALM

I CAN CONTROL MY CALM

MINDFUL MAZE

HOW ARE YOU FEELING?

REFLECT AND CONNECT

✋ Am I **H**ungry, **A**ntsy, **L**onely, **T**ired?

- What can I do?

READY TO RETURN_____ **NEED MORE TIME**_____

Draw or write what you are feeling.

What made you happy today?

-
-
-

reset my mindset

TODAY: _____

Circle the day:

MONDAY TUESDAY WEDNESDAY THURSDAY FRIDAY
SATURDAY SUNDAY

What time is it? _____

SET A TIMER

 5 mins

 3 mins  10 mins

BEGIN TO BREATHE

- Shoulders Still
- Breathe in
- Breathe out
- Trace the rainbow

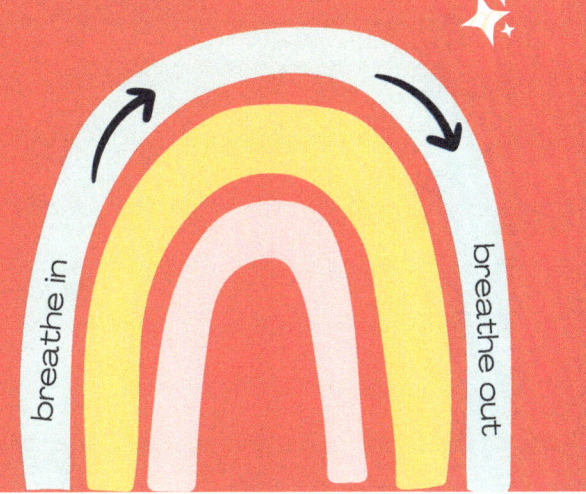

READ, COLOR, CALM

I CAN CONTROL MY CALM

MINDFUL MAZE

HOW ARE YOU FEELING?

REFLECT AND CONNECT

✋ Am I **H**ungry, **A**ntsy, **L**onely, **T**ired?

- What can I do?

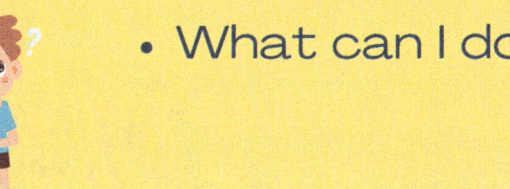

READY TO RETURN _____   NEED MORE TIME _____

Draw or write what you are feeling.

What made you happy today?

-
-
-

reset my mindset

TODAY: _____

Circle the day:

MONDAY TUESDAY WEDNESDAY THURSDAY FRIDAY
SATURDAY SUNDAY

What time is it? _____

SET A TIMER

 5 mins

 3 mins  10 mins

BEGIN TO BREATHE

- Shoulders Still
- Breathe in
- Breathe out
- Trace the rainbow

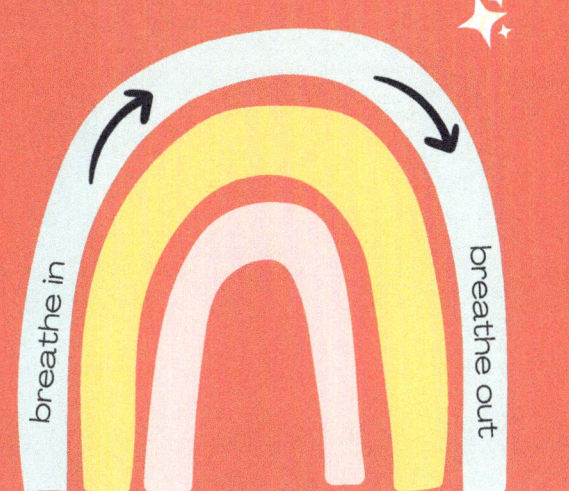

READ, COLOR, CALM

I CAN CONTROL MY CALM

MINDFUL MAZE

HOW ARE YOU FEELING?

REFLECT AND CONNECT

✋ Am I **H**ungry, **A**ntsy, **L**onely, **T**ired?

- What can I do?

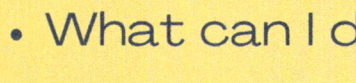

READY TO RETURN _____   NEED MORE TIME _____

Draw or write what you are feeling.

What made you happy today?

-
-
-

reset my mindset

TODAY: _____

Circle the day:

Monday   Tuesday   Wednesday   Thursday   Friday
Saturday   Sunday

What time is it? _____

SET A TIMER

 5 mins

 3 mins    10 mins

BEGIN TO BREATHE

- Shoulders Still
- Breathe in
- Breathe out
- Trace the rainbow

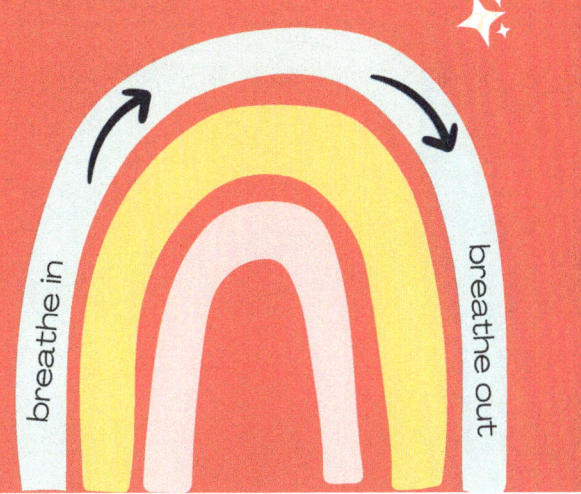

breathe in → breathe out

READ, COLOR, CALM

I CAN CONTROL MY CALM

MINDFUL MAZE

HOW ARE YOU FEELING?

REFLECT AND CONNECT

🖐 Am I **H**ungry, **A**ntsy, **L**onely, **T**ired?

- What can I do?

READY TO RETURN _____   NEED MORE TIME _____

Draw or write what you are feeling.

What made you happy today?

-
-
-

reset my mindset

TODAY: _____

Circle the day:

MONDAY   TUESDAY   WEDNESDAY   THURSDAY   FRIDAY
SATURDAY   SUNDAY

What time is it? _____

SET A TIMER

- 5 mins
- 3 mins
- 10 mins

BEGIN TO BREATHE

- Shoulders Still
- Breathe in
- Breathe out
- Trace the rainbow

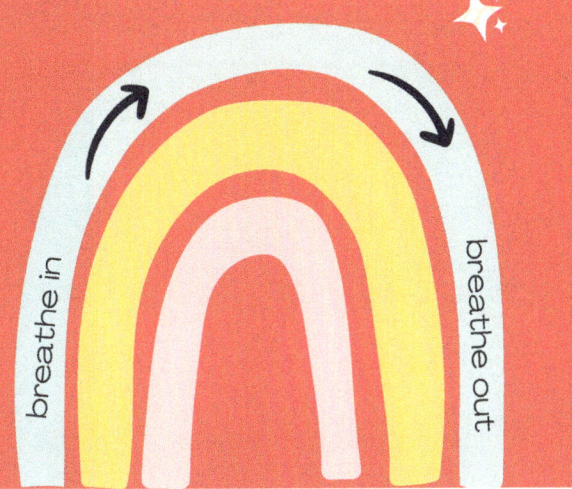

breathe in / breathe out

READ, COLOR, CALM

I CAN CONTROL MY CALM

MINDFUL MAZE

HOW ARE YOU FEELING?

REFLECT AND CONNECT

- Am I **H**ungry, **A**ntsy, **L**onely, **T**ired?
- What can I do?

READY TO RETURN _____   NEED MORE TIME _____

Draw or write what you are feeling.

What made you happy today?

-
-
-

reset my mindset

TODAY: _____

Circle the day:

MONDAY TUESDAY WEDNESDAY THURSDAY FRIDAY
SATURDAY SUNDAY

What time is it? _____

SET A TIMER

 5 mins

 3 mins  10 mins

BEGIN TO BREATHE

- Shoulders Still
- Breathe in
- Breathe out
- Trace the rainbow

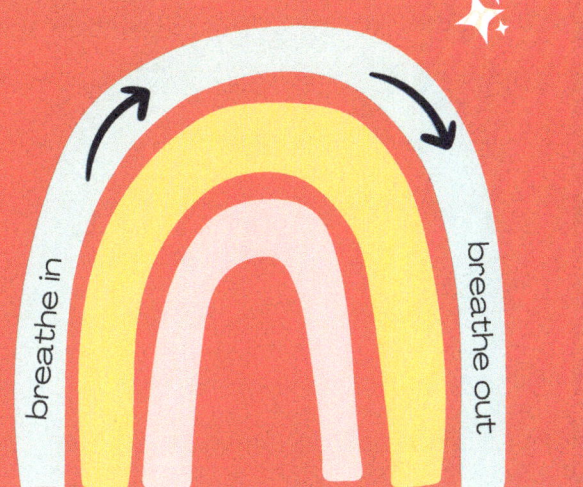

READ, COLOR, CALM

I CAN CONTROL MY CALM

MINDFUL MAZE

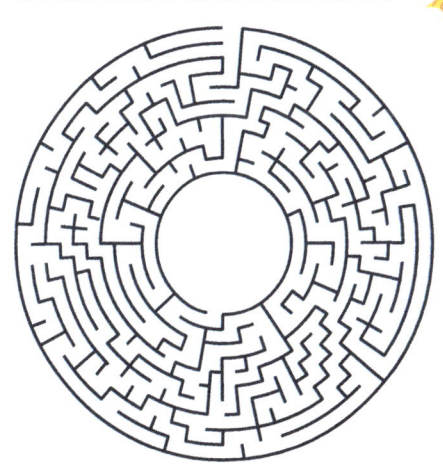

HOW ARE YOU FEELING?

REFLECT AND CONNECT

✋ Am I **H**ungry, **A**ntsy, **L**onely, **T**ired?

- What can I do?

READY TO RETURN _____   NEED MORE TIME _____

Draw or write what you are feeling.

What made you happy today?

-
-
-

reset my mindset

TODAY: _____

Circle the day:

MONDAY TUESDAY WEDNESDAY THURSDAY FRIDAY
SATURDAY SUNDAY

What time is it? _____

SET A TIMER

 5 mins
 3 mins    10 mins

BEGIN TO BREATHE

- Shoulders Still
- Breathe in
- Breathe out
- Trace the rainbow

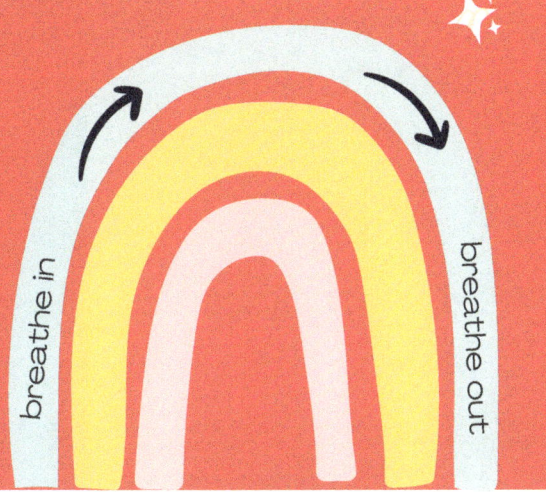

READ, COLOR, CALM

I CAN CONTROL MY CALM

MINDFUL MAZE

HOW ARE YOU FEELING?

REFLECT AND CONNECT

✋ Am I **H**ungry, **A**ntsy, **L**onely, **T**ired?

- What can I do?

READY TO RETURN _____   NEED MORE TIME _____

Draw or write what you are feeling.

What made you happy today?

-
-
-

reset my mindset

TODAY: _____

Circle the day:

MONDAY TUESDAY WEDNESDAY THURSDAY FRIDAY
SATURDAY SUNDAY

What time is it? _____

SET A TIMER

 5 mins

 3 mins  10 mins

BEGIN TO BREATHE

- Shoulders Still
- Breathe in
- Breathe out
- Trace the rainbow

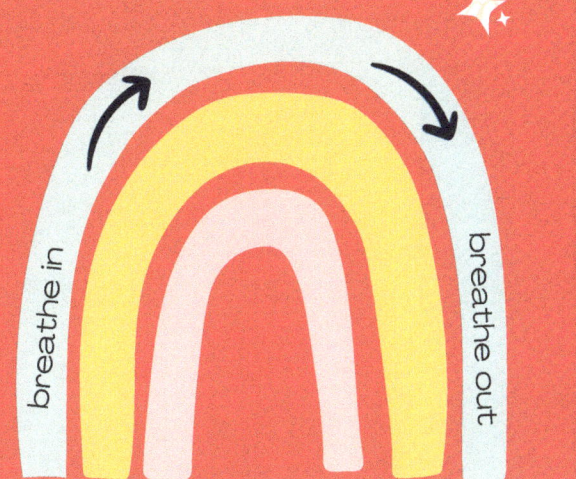

READ, COLOR, CALM

I CAN CONTROL MY CALM

MINDFUL MAZE

HOW ARE YOU FEELING?

REFLECT AND CONNECT

 Am I **H**ungry, **A**ntsy, **L**onely, **T**ired?

- What can I do?

READY TO RETURN _____   NEED MORE TIME _____

Draw or write what you are feeling.

What made you happy today?

-
-
-

reset my mindset

TODAY: _____

Circle the day:

MONDAY TUESDAY WEDNESDAY THURSDAY FRIDAY
SATURDAY SUNDAY

What time is it? _____

SET A TIMER

 5 mins

 3 mins  10 mins

BEGIN TO BREATHE

- Shoulders Still
- Breathe in
- Breathe out
- Trace the rainbow

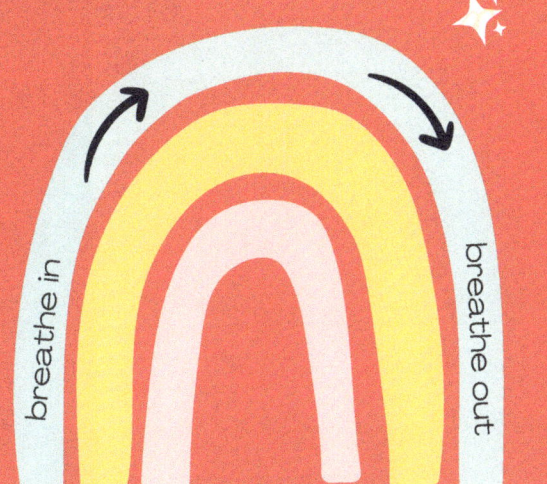

READ, COLOR, CALM

I CAN CONTROL MY CALM

MINDFUL MAZE

HOW ARE YOU FEELING?

REFLECT AND CONNECT

- Am I **H**ungry, **A**ntsy, **L**onely, **T**ired?
- What can I do?

READY TO RETURN _____   NEED MORE TIME _____

Draw or write what you are feeling.

What made you happy today?

-
-
-

reset my mindset

TODAY: _____

Circle the day:

Monday **Tuesday** **Wednesday** **Thursday** **Friday**
Saturday **Sunday**

What time is it? _____

SET A TIMER

 5 mins

 3 mins  10 mins

BEGIN TO BREATHE

- Shoulders Still
- Breathe in
- Breathe out
- Trace the rainbow

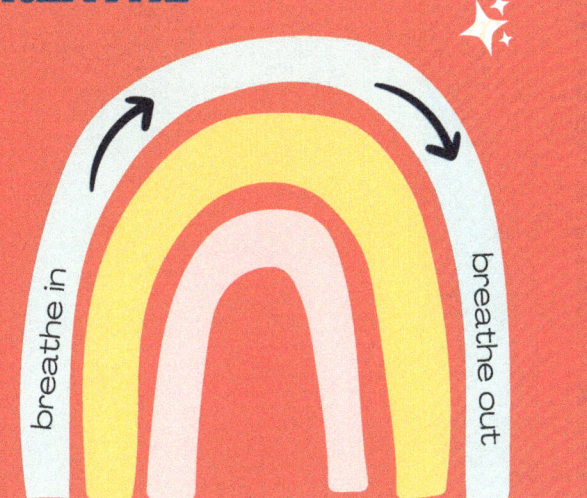

breathe in — breathe out

READ, COLOR, CALM

I CAN CONTROL MY CALM

MINDFUL MAZE

HOW ARE YOU FEELING?

REFLECT AND CONNECT

🤚 Am I **H**ungry, **A**ntsy, **L**onely, **T**ired?

- What can I do?

READY TO RETURN _____   NEED MORE TIME _____

Draw or write what you are feeling.

What made you happy today?

-
-
-

reset my mindset

TODAY: _____

Circle the day:

MONDAY TUESDAY WEDNESDAY THURSDAY FRIDAY
SATURDAY SUNDAY

What time is it? _____

SET A TIMER

- 5 mins
- 3 mins
- 10 mins

BEGIN TO BREATHE

- Shoulders Still
- Breathe in
- Breathe out
- Trace the rainbow

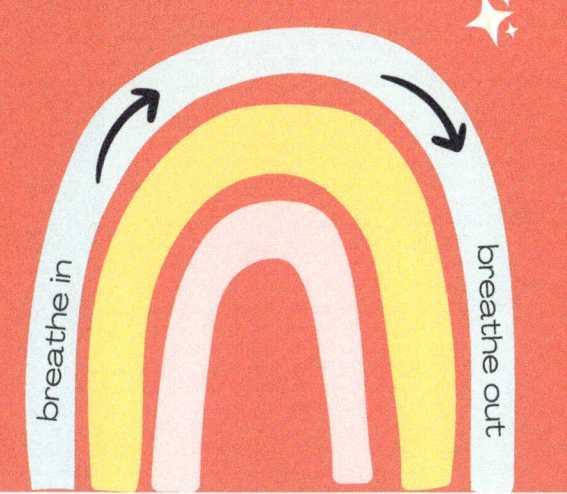

READ, COLOR, CALM

I CAN CONTROL MY CALM

MINDFUL MAZE

HOW ARE YOU FEELING?

REFLECT AND CONNECT

- Am I **H**ungry, **A**ntsy, **L**onely, **T**ired?
- What can I do?

READY TO RETURN _____   NEED MORE TIME _____

Draw or write what you are feeling.

What made you happy today?

-
-
-

reset my mindset

TODAY: _____

Circle the day:

MONDAY TUESDAY WEDNESDAY THURSDAY FRIDAY
SATURDAY SUNDAY

What time is it? _____

SET A TIMER

 5 mins

 3 mins  10 mins

BEGIN TO BREATHE

- Shoulders Still
- Breathe in
- Breathe out
- Trace the rainbow

READ, COLOR, CALM

I CAN CONTROL MY CALM

MINDFUL MAZE

HOW ARE YOU FEELING?

REFLECT AND CONNECT

- Am I **H**ungry, **A**ntsy, **L**onely, **T**ired?
- What can I do?

READY TO RETURN _____   NEED MORE TIME _____

Draw or write what you are feeling.

What made you happy today?

-
-
-

reset my mindset

TODAY: _____

Circle the day:

MONDAY TUESDAY WEDNESDAY THURSDAY FRIDAY
SATURDAY SUNDAY

What time is it? _____

SET A TIMER

 5 mins

 3 mins    10 mins

BEGIN TO BREATHE

- Shoulders Still
- Breathe in
- Breathe out
- Trace the rainbow

READ, COLOR, CALM

I CAN CONTROL MY CALM

MINDFUL MAZE

HOW ARE YOU FEELING?

REFLECT AND CONNECT

✋ Am I **H**ungry, **A**ntsy, **L**onely, **T**ired?

- What can I do?

READY TO RETURN _____   NEED MORE TIME _____

Draw or write what you are feeling.

What made you happy today?

-
-
-

reset my mindset

TODAY: _____

Circle the day:

MONDAY TUESDAY WEDNESDAY THURSDAY FRIDAY
SATURDAY SUNDAY

What time is it?_____

SET A TIMER

 5 mins

 3 mins  10 mins

BEGIN TO BREATHE

- Shoulders Still
- Breathe in
- Breathe out
- Trace the rainbow

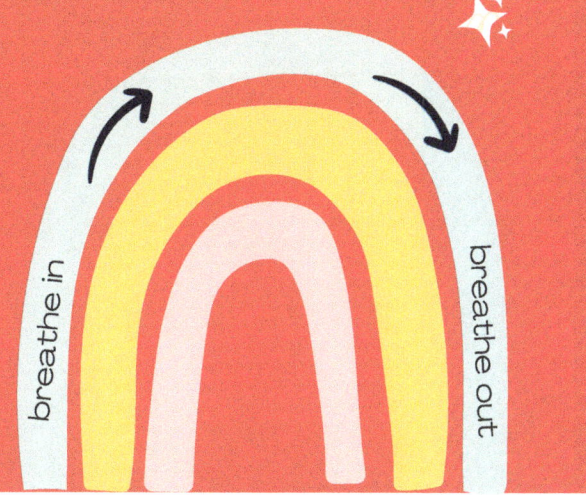
breathe in / breathe out

READ, COLOR, CALM

I CAN CONTROL MY CALM

MINDFUL MAZE

HOW ARE YOU FEELING?

REFLECT AND CONNECT

✋ Am I **H**ungry, **A**ntsy, **L**onely, **T**ired?

- What can I do?

READY TO RETURN _____   **NEED MORE TIME** _____

Draw or write what you are feeling.

What made you happy today?

-
-
-

reset my mindset

TODAY: _____

Circle the day:

MONDAY TUESDAY WEDNESDAY THURSDAY FRIDAY
SATURDAY SUNDAY

What time is it? _____

SET A TIMER

 5 mins

 3 mins  10 mins

BEGIN TO BREATHE

- Shoulders Still
- Breathe in
- Breathe out
- Trace the rainbow

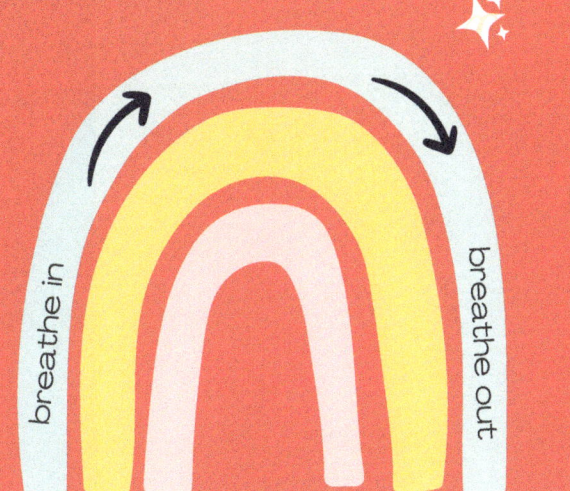

breathe in / breathe out

READ, COLOR, CALM

I CAN CONTROL MY CALM

MINDFUL MAZE

HOW ARE YOU FEELING?

REFLECT AND CONNECT

🤚 Am I **H**ungry, **A**ntsy, **L**onely, **T**ired?

- What can I do?

READY TO RETURN _____   NEED MORE TIME _____

Draw or write what you are feeling.

What made you happy today?

-
-
-

reset my mindset

TODAY: _____

Circle the day:

MONDAY TUESDAY WEDNESDAY THURSDAY FRIDAY
SATURDAY SUNDAY

What time is it?_____

SET A TIMER

- 5 mins
- 3 mins
- 10 mins

BEGIN TO BREATHE

- Shoulders Still
- Breathe in
- Breathe out
- Trace the rainbow

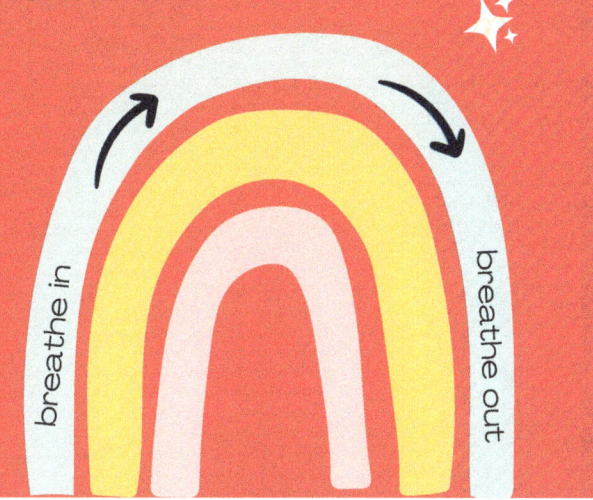

breathe in → breathe out

READ, COLOR, CALM

I CAN CONTROL MY CALM

MINDFUL MAZE

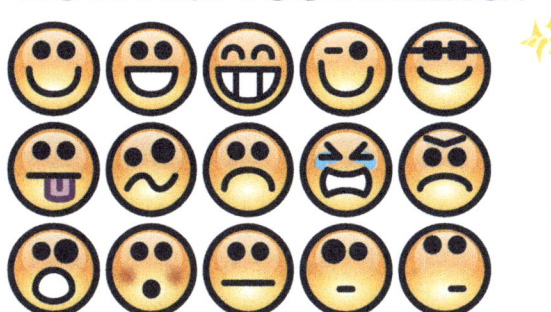

HOW ARE YOU FEELING?

REFLECT AND CONNECT

- Am I **H**ungry, **A**ntsy, **L**onely, **T**ired?
- What can I do?

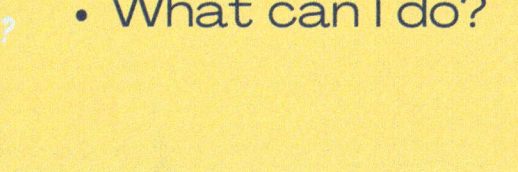

READY TO RETURN _____   NEED MORE TIME _____

Draw or write what you are feeling.

What made you happy today?

-
-
-

BE KIND TO YOUR MIND

reset my mindset

TODAY: _____

Circle the day:

MONDAY   TUESDAY   WEDNESDAY   THURSDAY   FRIDAY
SATURDAY   SUNDAY

What time is it?_____

SET A TIMER
- 5 mins
- 3 mins
- 10 mins

BEGIN TO BREATHE
- Shoulders Still
- Breathe in
- Breathe out
- Trace the rainbow

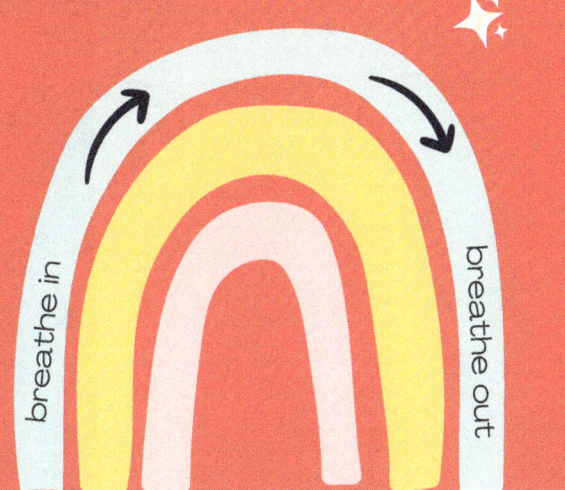

breathe in → breathe out

READ, COLOR, CALM
I CAN CONTROL MY CALM

MINDFUL MAZE

HOW ARE YOU FEELING?

REFLECT AND CONNECT
- Am I **H**ungry, **A**ntsy, **L**onely, **T**ired?
- What can I do?

READY TO RETURN_____   NEED MORE TIME_____

Draw or write what you are feeling.

What made you happy today?

-
-
-

BE KIND TO YOUR MIND

reset my mindset

TODAY: _____

Circle the day:

MONDAY   TUESDAY   WEDNESDAY   THURSDAY   FRIDAY
SATURDAY   SUNDAY

What time is it? _____

SET A TIMER

- 5 mins
- 3 mins
- 10 mins

BEGIN TO BREATHE

- Shoulders Still
- Breathe in
- Breathe out
- Trace the rainbow

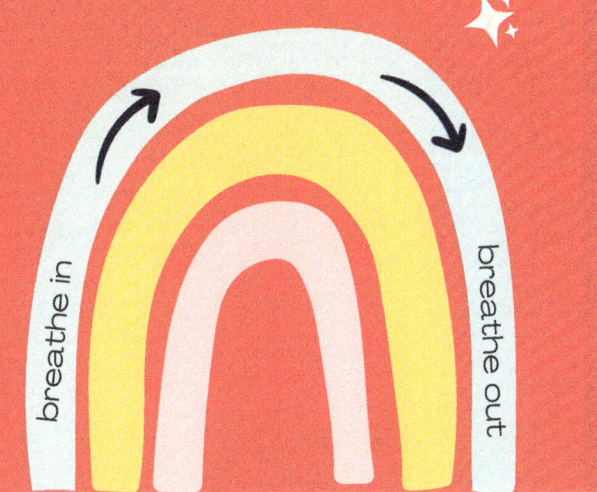

breathe in → breathe out

READ, COLOR, CALM

I CAN CONTROL MY CALM

MINDFUL MAZE

HOW ARE YOU FEELING?

REFLECT AND CONNECT

Am I **H**ungry, **A**ntsy, **L**onely, **T**ired?

- What can I do?

READY TO RETURN _____   NEED MORE TIME _____

Draw or write what you are feeling.

What made you happy today?

-
-
-

BE KIND TO YOUR MIND

reset my mindset

TODAY: _____

Circle the day:

MONDAY TUESDAY WEDNESDAY THURSDAY FRIDAY
SATURDAY SUNDAY

What time is it? _____

SET A TIMER

- 5 mins
- 3 mins
- 10 mins

BEGIN TO BREATHE

- Shoulders Still
- Breathe in
- Breathe out
- Trace the rainbow

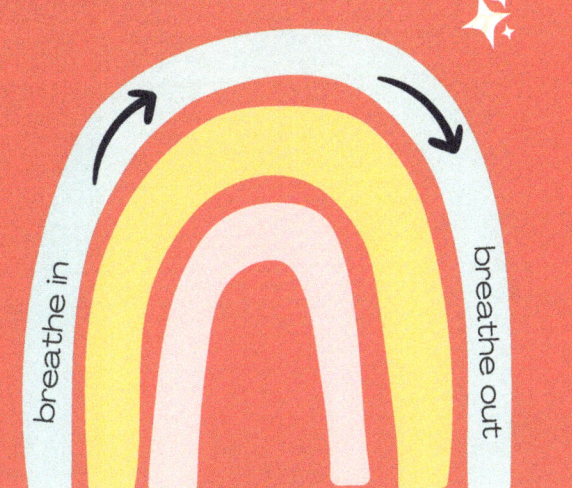

breathe in → breathe out

READ, COLOR, CALM

I CAN CONTROL MY CALM

MINDFUL MAZE

HOW ARE YOU FEELING?

REFLECT AND CONNECT

- Am I **H**ungry, **A**ntsy, **L**onely, **T**ired?
- What can I do?

READY TO RETURN _____   NEED MORE TIME _____

Draw or write what you are feeling.

What made you happy today?

-
-
-

BE KIND TO YOUR MIND

reset my mindset

TODAY: _____

Circle the day:

MONDAY   TUESDAY   WEDNESDAY   THURSDAY   FRIDAY
SATURDAY   SUNDAY

What time is it? _____

SET A TIMER

- 5 mins
- 3 mins
- 10 mins

BEGIN TO BREATHE

- Shoulders Still
- Breathe in
- Breathe out
- Trace the rainbow

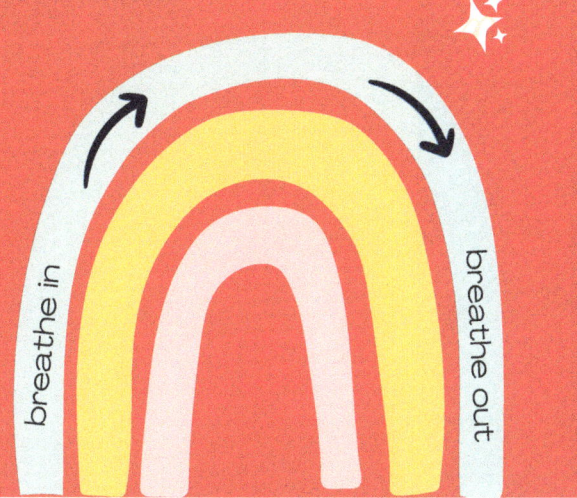

breathe in → breathe out

READ, COLOR, CALM

I CAN CONTROL MY CALM

MINDFUL MAZE

HOW ARE YOU FEELING?

REFLECT AND CONNECT

Am I **H**ungry, **A**ntsy, **L**onely, **T**ired?

- What can I do?

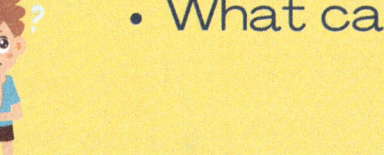

READY TO RETURN _____   NEED MORE TIME _____

Draw or write what you are feeling.

What made you happy today?

-
-
-

Be Kind To Your Mind

reset my mindset

TODAY: _____

Circle the day:

Monday   Tuesday   Wednesday   Thursday   Friday
Saturday   Sunday

What time is it? _____

SET A TIMER

- 5 mins
- 3 mins
- 10 mins

BEGIN TO BREATHE

- Shoulders Still
- Breathe in
- Breathe out
- Trace the rainbow

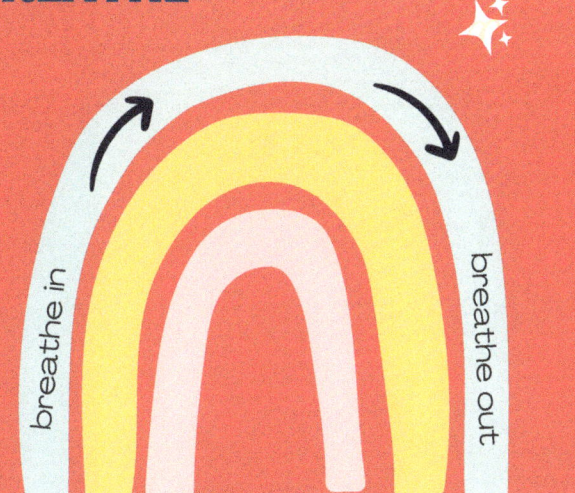

breathe in → breathe out

READ, COLOR, CALM

I CAN CONTROL MY CALM

MINDFUL MAZE

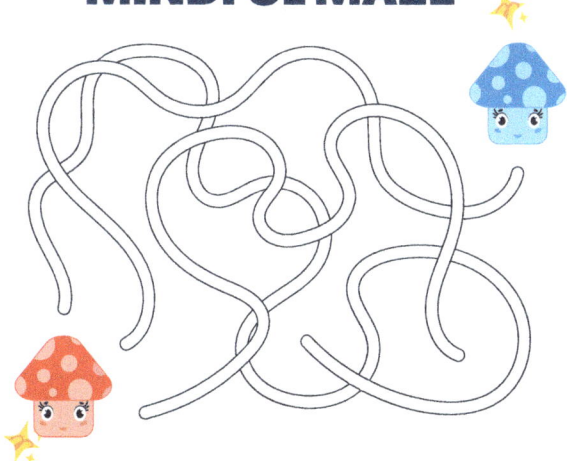

HOW ARE YOU FEELING?

REFLECT AND CONNECT

- Am I **H**ungry, **A**ntsy, **L**onely, **T**ired?
- What can I do?

READY TO RETURN _____   NEED MORE TIME _____

Draw or write what you are feeling.

What made you happy today?

-
-
-

BE KIND TO YOUR MIND

reset my mindset

TODAY: _____

Circle the day:

Monday   Tuesday   Wednesday   Thursday   Friday
Saturday   Sunday

What time is it? _____

SET A TIMER
- 5 mins
- 3 mins
- 10 mins

BEGIN TO BREATHE
- Shoulders Still
- Breathe in
- Breathe out
- Trace the rainbow

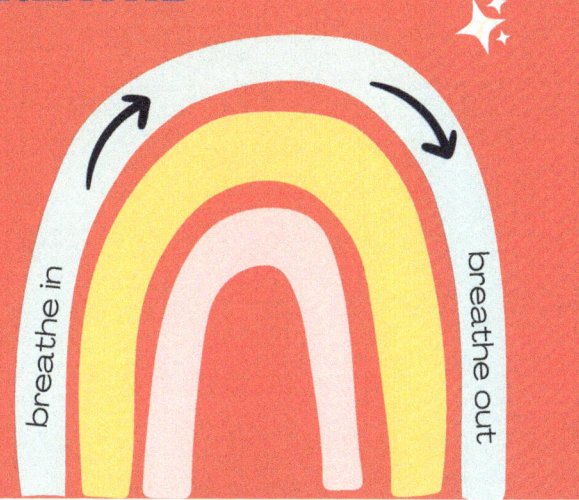

breathe in → breathe out

READ, COLOR, CALM
I CAN CONTROL MY CALM

MINDFUL MAZE

HOW ARE YOU FEELING?

REFLECT AND CONNECT
- Am I **H**ungry, **A**ntsy, **L**onely, **T**ired?
- What can I do?

READY TO RETURN _____   NEED MORE TIME _____

Draw or write what you are feeling.

What made you happy today?

-
-
-

BE KIND TO YOUR MIND

reset my mindset

TODAY: _____

Circle the day:

Monday Tuesday Wednesday Thursday Friday
Saturday Sunday

What time is it? _____

SET A TIMER

- 5 mins
- 3 mins
- 10 mins

BEGIN TO BREATHE

- Shoulders Still
- Breathe in
- Breathe out
- Trace the rainbow

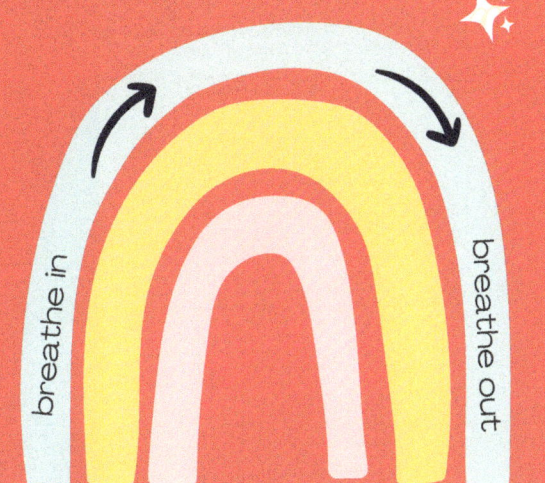

breathe in → breathe out

READ, COLOR, CALM

I CAN CONTROL MY CALM

MINDFUL MAZE

HOW ARE YOU FEELING?

REFLECT AND CONNECT

- Am I **H**ungry, **A**ntsy, **L**onely, **T**ired?
- What can I do?

READY TO RETURN _____   NEED MORE TIME _____

Draw or write what you are feeling.

What made you happy today?

-
-
-

Be Kind To Your Mind

reset my mindset

TODAY: _____

Circle the day:

Monday **Tuesday** **Wednesday** **Thursday** **Friday**
Saturday **Sunday**

What time is it? _____

SET A TIMER

- 5 mins
- 3 mins
- 10 mins

BEGIN TO BREATHE

- Shoulders Still
- Breathe in
- Breathe out
- Trace the rainbow

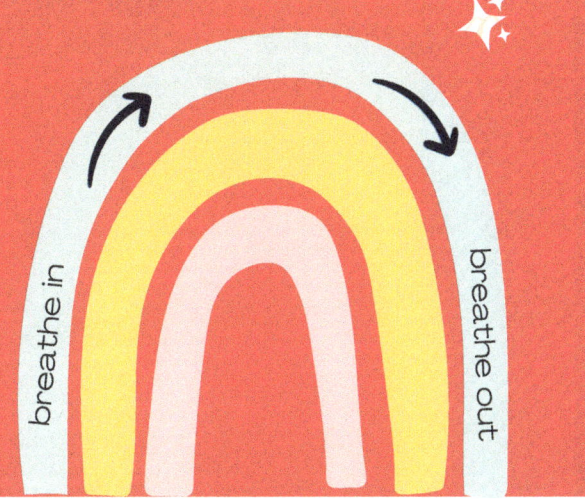

breathe in → breathe out

READ, COLOR, CALM

I CAN CONTROL MY CALM

MINDFUL MAZE

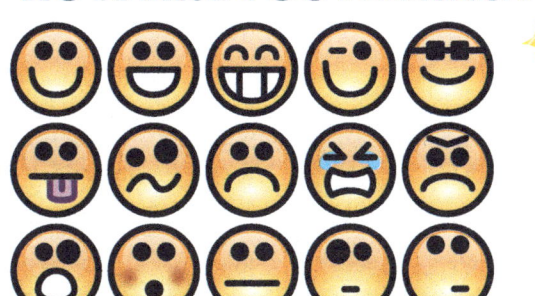

HOW ARE YOU FEELING?

REFLECT AND CONNECT

- Am I **H**ungry, **A**ntsy, **L**onely, **T**ired?
- What can I do?

READY TO RETURN _____   NEED MORE TIME _____

Draw or write what you are feeling.

What made you happy today?

-
-
-

BE KIND TO YOUR MIND

reset my mindset

TODAY: _____

Circle the day:

**MONDAY   TUESDAY   WEDNESDAY   THURSDAY   FRIDAY
SATURDAY   SUNDAY**

What time is it? _____

SET A TIMER
- 5 mins
- 3 mins
- 10 mins

BEGIN TO BREATHE
- Shoulders Still
- Breathe in
- Breathe out
- Trace the rainbow

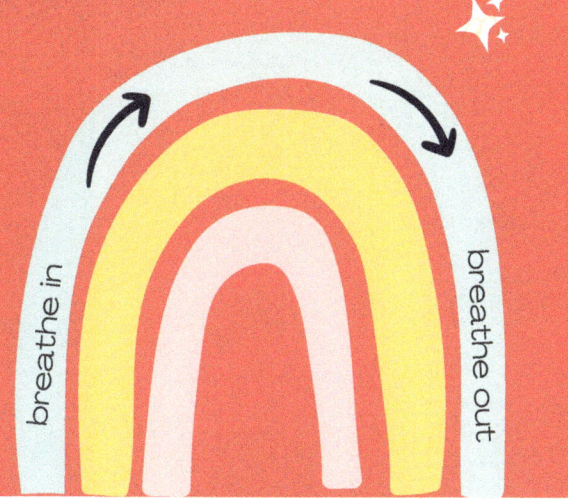

breathe in → breathe out

READ, COLOR, CALM

I CAN CONTROL MY CALM

MINDFUL MAZE

HOW ARE YOU FEELING?

REFLECT AND CONNECT

Am I **H**ungry, **A**ntsy, **L**onely, **T**ired?
- What can I do?

READY TO RETURN _____   **NEED MORE TIME** _____

Draw or write what you are feeling.

What made you happy today?

-
-
-

Be kind to your mind

reset my mindset

TODAY: _____

Circle the day:

MONDAY   TUESDAY   WEDNESDAY   THURSDAY   FRIDAY
SATURDAY   SUNDAY

What time is it? _____

SET A TIMER

- 5 mins
- 3 mins
- 10 mins

BEGIN TO BREATHE

- Shoulders Still
- Breathe in
- Breathe out
- Trace the rainbow

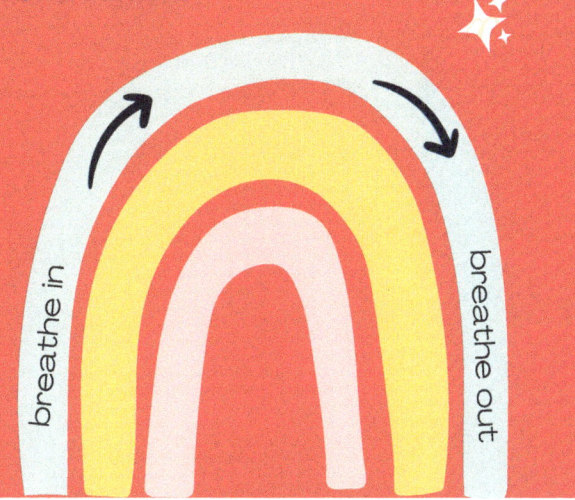

breathe in → ← breathe out

READ, COLOR, CALM

I CAN CONTROL MY CALM

MINDFUL MAZE

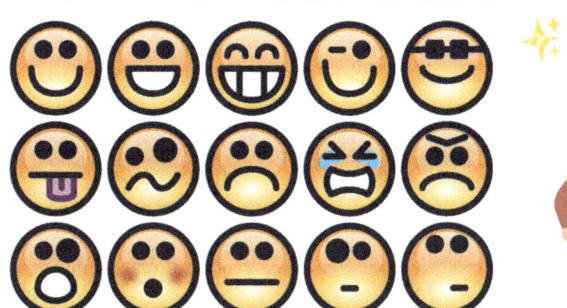

HOW ARE YOU FEELING?

REFLECT AND CONNECT

✋ Am I **H**ungry, **A**ntsy, **L**onely, **T**ired?

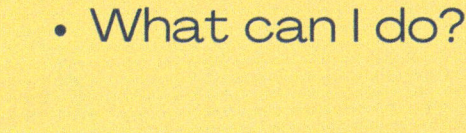

- What can I do?

READY TO RETURN _____   NEED MORE TIME _____

Draw or write what you are feeling.

What made you happy today?

-
-
-

BE KIND TO YOUR MIND

reset my mindset

TODAY: _____

Circle the day:

**Monday Tuesday Wednesday Thursday Friday
Saturday Sunday**

What time is it? _____

SET A TIMER

- 5 mins
- 3 mins
- 10 mins

BEGIN TO BREATHE

- Shoulders Still
- Breathe in
- Breathe out
- Trace the rainbow

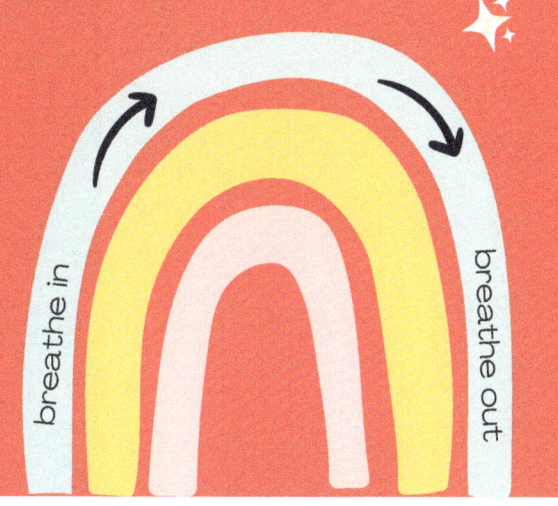

breathe in → breathe out

READ, COLOR, CALM

I CAN CONTROL MY CALM

MINDFUL MAZE

HOW ARE YOU FEELING?

REFLECT AND CONNECT

- Am I **H**ungry, **A**ntsy, **L**onely, **T**ired?
- What can I do?

READY TO RETURN _____   NEED MORE TIME _____

Draw or write what you are feeling.

What made you happy today?

-
-
-

BE KIND TO YOUR MIND

reset my mindset

TODAY: _____

Circle the day:

MONDAY TUESDAY WEDNESDAY THURSDAY FRIDAY
SATURDAY SUNDAY

What time is it?_____

SET A TIMER

- 5 mins
- 3 mins
- 10 mins

BEGIN TO BREATHE

- Shoulders Still
- Breathe in
- Breathe out
- Trace the rainbow

breathe in — breathe out

READ, COLOR, CALM

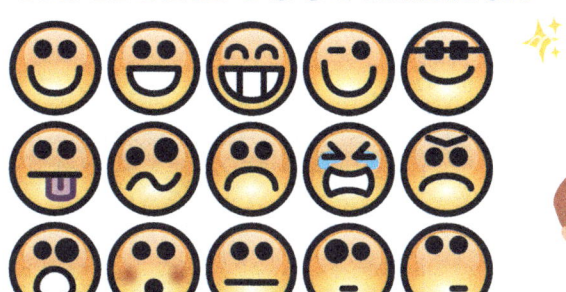

I CAN CONTROL MY CALM

MINDFUL MAZE

HOW ARE YOU FEELING?

REFLECT AND CONNECT

- Am I **H**ungry, **A**ntsy, **L**onely, **T**ired?
- What can I do?

READY TO RETURN _____   NEED MORE TIME _____

Draw or write what you are feeling.

What made you happy today?

-
-
-

BE KIND TO YOUR MIND

reset my mindset

TODAY: _____

Circle the day:

MONDAY TUESDAY WEDNESDAY THURSDAY FRIDAY
SATURDAY SUNDAY

What time is it? _____

SET A TIMER

- 5 mins
- 3 mins
- 10 mins

BEGIN TO BREATHE

- Shoulders Still
- Breathe in
- Breathe out
- Trace the rainbow

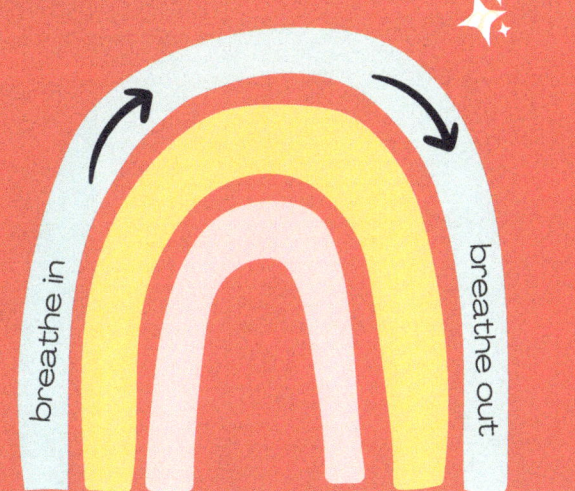

breathe in → breathe out

READ, COLOR, CALM

I CAN CONTROL MY CALM

MINDFUL MAZE

HOW ARE YOU FEELING?

REFLECT AND CONNECT

- Am I **H**ungry, **A**ntsy, **L**onely, **T**ired?
- What can I do?

READY TO RETURN _____   NEED MORE TIME _____

Draw or write what you are feeling.

What made you happy today?

-
-
-

BE KIND TO YOUR MIND

You Got This.

but need a little more?

- ▶ Stand, move, or take a walk.

- ▶ Use an anchor phrase. "I'm (name), I'm (x) years old and live in (city/state)". Repeat.

- ▶ Play brain games, puzzles, bubbles, or build.

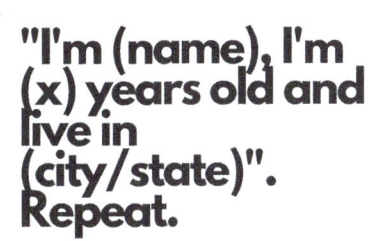

- ▶ Drink water, wash your hands or hold ice.

- ▶ Focus on a song or sound (try brown noise).

- ▶ Make a fist, hold and release, letting your feelings go too.

You Got This.

Make a list! What helps you find your calm?

▶
▶

▶
▶

▶
▶

▶

You Got This.

DOODLE AND DRAW!

You Got This.

DOODLE AND DRAW!

You Got This.

DOODLE AND DRAW!

You Got This.

DOODLE AND DRAW!

You Got This.

DOODLE AND DRAW!

You Got This.

DOODLE AND DRAW!

Made in the USA
Monee, IL
09 September 2023